# Poetic Insights

## Laura Buck

Trilogy Christian Publishers

A Wholly Owned Subsidiary of Trinity Broadcasting Network

2442 Michelle Drive

Tustin, CA 92780

Copyright © 2023 by Laura Buck

All rights reserved, including the right to reproduce this book or portions thereof in any form whatsoever.

For information, address Trilogy Christian Publishing

Rights Department, 2442 Michelle Drive, Tustin, CA 92780.

Trilogy Christian Publishing/TBN and colophon are trademarks of Trinity Broadcasting Network.

For information about special discounts for bulk purchases, please contact Trilogy Christian Publishing.

Manufactured in the United States of America

Trilogy Disclaimer: The views and content expressed in this book are those of the author and may not necessarily reflect the views and doctrine of Trilogy Christian Publishing or the Trinity Broadcasting Network.

10 9 8 7 6 5 4 3 2 1

Library of Congress Cataloging-in-Publication Data is available.

ISBN 979-8-89041-444-1

ISBN (ebook) 979-8-89041-445-8

# Dedication

To my twin flame

*always and forever*

# Foreword

I feel I was divinely inspired to write this book of poems. I received enlightened words of encouragement, which ignited a flame to burn inside me. I *hope* the transparent poetic verses light a spark within you, to see there is light in the dark.

# Preface

## "Speak your truth, and let the voice of your heart be heard."

(Words spoken to me a year prior to writing this book)

# Acknowledgments

I am so grateful for my dearly loved family and friends!

**Bobby**, I *love* you with all my heart! You have been by my side and continue to always love me wholeheartedly. Writing this book, I feel, brought us closer together. You are my soulmate; the twinkle that sparkles in your eyes when you look at me is all I need! I know you see me.

**Kyler and Brayden**, you both have always been my light in my darkest hour. You both are my purpose in life, and I'm so proud of the individuals you are growing up to be. Always chase after your dreams! I hope I've anchored you with the *love* and encouragement needed to always feel brave enough to follow your hearts. Never lose sight of the fire that burns in your souls. I *love* you with all my heart!

**Kara**, you ignited a flame to burn inside me. Without you, I never would have written this book. You believed in me when I needed *hope*. Thank you! I *love* you!

**Thomas**, you are my silent serenity. We have a special bond that I will cherish forever! You are a bright light in my life! Never stop glowing! I *love* you!

**Joe**, you understand me on a level that can't be described in words. You are my first best friend, who has always been there for me when I needed someone to listen. You give the best advice that I will cherish forever! I *love* you!

***Mom and Dad***, thank you for always listening and being supportive. Thank you for telling me you're proud of me! Hearing those words are the best coming from my loving parents that I adore with all my heart! I *love* you!

***Bob and Debbie***, thank you for raising such a wonderful son, whom I love with all my heart! Your *love* for me shines bright every time we see each other. Thank you for being you! I *love* you both very much!

***Grandma Bonnie***, you hold such a dear spot in my heart! You have always given me so much *love* and support in my life! I appreciate you so much! Thank you for everything you have done for me and my family, and for helping raise the boys. I *love* you!

***Grandpa Larry***, you have always been such an encouragement in my life! I always feel you believe in me, which gives me *hope* and inspiration! I *love* you!

***Aunt Mary***, you are such a bright, beautiful soul! You always have been a loving support, any time I need advice. You mean the world to me. I *love* you so much!

***Alvina, Angie, and Sheri***, you three are my soul tribe; you three make me feel so happy and loved! Trusted friends I will always know with all my heart that believe in me, and are real beautiful souls! You brighten this dark world with your light! ***Never stop shining***!!

# Introduction

*Poetic Insight* is a profound assortment of poems that wholeheartedly exhilarate true sentimental feelings of heartbreak and passion. Dive into these captivating words of true inspiration, translating raw, emotional feelings of pain written so transparently you'll feel yourself interweave through the rhythmic insight, healing your soul with these impacting words of *guidance, love and hope.*

It begins with a broken soul finding her way. As you follow her through her journey, she finds tranquility and peacefulness lifting her in her darkest moments.

Never give up hope; love is always willing to comfort you and embrace you during your most vulnerable stages you endure during your passage of life.

Open your eyes to the beauty all around you, if you listen closely enough you can hear the soft whispers of reassurance, calming your soul with *graceful sovereignty.*

# Contents

Eyes Wide Open ....................................................... 1

Glowworm ............................................................. 2

Intuition ............................................................ 3

Shattered Soul ....................................................... 4

Heart Strings ........................................................ 5

Broken ............................................................... 6

Tormented Torture .................................................... 7

Flight ............................................................... 9

Insomnia ............................................................. 10

Decay ................................................................ 11

Saving Grace ......................................................... 12

Hope ................................................................. 14

Patina ............................................................... 15

Spirit ............................................................... 16

Daydream ............................................................. 18

Window ............................................................... 19

Embrace .............................................................. 20

Found ................................................................ 21

Treasure Chest ....................................................... 22

Endless Chatter ...................................................... 23

Unconditional ........................................................ 24

Let Go ............................................................... 25

Shine Bright ......................................................... 26

Synchronicity ............................................. 27
Soul Sister ............................................... 28
Calm ..................................................... 29
Twin Flame ............................................... 30
Soul Mate ................................................ 32
Wedding Day ............................................. 33
You ...................................................... 35
Me ....................................................... 36
Little Sis ................................................. 37
Mama & Papa ............................................ 39
Silent Serenity ........................................... 40
Cleanse .................................................. 41
Reflect ................................................... 42
Inspire ................................................... 43
MoonDance Mirage ....................................... 44
Golden Light ............................................. 45
Life ...................................................... 46
Life Path # 7 ............................................. 48
Magical Adventure ....................................... 50
Twilight .................................................. 52
Vow ...................................................... 54
Rebirth .................................................. 55
Divine ................................................... 56
All As One ............................................... 57
Sixth Sense .............................................. 59
Buried Alive ............................................. 60
Epilogue ................................................. 61
About The Author ........................................ 62

# Eyes Wide Open

I know you can't be me.
I wish you could; I'd make it be,
but all I can do is explain to you
so here I go, my words are few,
all I want is to be *seen*,
so look through my eyes
will you please?
Come inside, enjoy the view,
your understanding will become anew,
all I want is to be *heard*,
take my ears and listen to my words,
dance to the rhythm of my beat.
It sounds pretty good, don't you think?
All I want is to be *understood* the most,
take my heart and hold it close,
come inside and be my *host*.

*Poetic Insights*

# Glowworm

The answers you wonder are deep inside
all you have to do is read my rhyme,
I feel my heart is on my sleeve
but better yet an *open book* for all to read.
Each verse I write from my soul
so please read my words
and make me *glow*,
study my penmanship that I write down,
devour my verslet so I don't break down,
my open book is anxiously waiting to be heard,
dive right in and be captivated by my word.
I needed to be rekindled for my light to *shine bright*,
I'm full of emotions and thoughts inside.
Please read my words I've written and provide
all the emotions I feel are
translated to expressions,
terms and phrases,
I dream of the day I receive your *praises*!

# Intuition

*I* can feel fakeness to the core of my bones
words unspoken
sight be known,
*I* can see in body language,
and when you walked away in times of need,
and when you tried to walk back to me I'd already seen,
we know the unknown
and see the unseen,
you can't fool *empathic genes*,
we see things clearly,
clear as can be,
we feel with our hearts
encased with *emotions severely*,
my light needs to shine in this dark dreadful scene,
if I had to do it all over again,
I'd speak the same words spoken,
I would stand up with reason
and *speak* the truth brave enough needed to be spoken,
casting my truth without words being broken.
I'd do it all over again
without hesitation,
speaking my truth
my *truthful explanation.*

# Shattered Soul

Suffocating emotions take hold from within
pulling me down this path where I've been.
Standing alone,
slowly defeated and worn,
numbness creeps inside me
tearing me with thorns.
Trembling inside
blurred pictures play in my mind,
constantly beating me
dripping with despair,
needing to feel *love*
but receiving life's gift that's unfair.
Desperation is too strong
I'm being overtaken,
shattering me to pieces
my *love* is forsaken.

# Heart Strings

I want to sing
in perfect harmony
in your attuning heart,
but your ears fall deaf
from my stale inaudible
voice box of
discordant heartache.

# Broken

I thought a broken heart was a figure of speech.
No, that's wrong, I feel mine breaking inside me,
the brokenness is something I cannot hide
it feels so horrible I want to die.
I need someone
to pick up my broken pieces
to love me,
*save me,*
my heart is speechless.
I have a soul that is shattered and torn,
I lay here broken and worn,
my heart is heavy; it's hard to breathe,
please don't let me fall beneath,
the chest pains are starting,
*"What do I do?"*
Please help me,
save me,
make me *brand new*.

# Tormented Torture

When I was young I was bullied and teased
the harsh words making me freeze,
I was chased with dead snakes
and threatened to be beat up,
GOD, please help me
*save me,*
tell me where to meet up!
I was tall and thin
and stood out,
but this is me, so let me go about.
I tried my best to move on with my worth
but can I possibly have a re-birth?
I was made fun of
poked and mocked,
in exchange I locked my heart up from the feelings
that it knocked,

*Poetic Insights*

I was ridiculed for reasons unclear
all these emotions I can't truly bear,
if you don't like me
just leave me alone,
but I ask please don't treat me wrongly,
I want to go *home*.

# Flight

Sitting along the rocky cliff edge,
imagining feathers being grown
saving me from falling death,
contemplating with strife,
thinking with all of my might,
*"Where do I go?"*
"What do I do with my life?"
I want to grow wings and learn how to fly,
to jump without hesitation,
and glide through the night,
to float in the breeze with pure *peace* in my wings,
soar through the trees
and dive with ease,
feeling alive
letting go of fear.
Is that hope I hear whispering in my ear?
So I give you my pain and pray,
GOD, please make me
a *bird someday*.

# Insomnia

I wait for you inside our room and pray,
alone in our bed thinking of the day,
I ask you to come with me,
and you say,
*"No, thanks I'm better off, okay?"*
you feel so distant,
How can we go on this way?
I can't be with you
if you push me away,
I need someone to hold me close,
to be my *savior*
and happy dose,
I need to be held and handled with care,
but all I receive is a blank stare,
I need someone with an essence,
a *beautiful soul*,
to encase me with their presence
and make me *whole*.

# Decay

I can feel my lungs breathing in and out,
every breath in,
and every breath out,
yet I feel like nothing just a deteriorating shell,
my body is screaming
*"Where are you now?"*
*"I'm floating above you,*
*I want out! When I'm inside you I feel*
*withered, shattered, and torn,*
*you make me feel broken, smashed, and sore,*
*so leave me be, body*
*I'm going away,*
*heaven is above me anticipating my stay,*
*it's bright and beautiful full of love,*
*that's where I'm going*
*to the serene beauty above."*

# Saving Grace

Hoping the flooding thoughts will soon cease
and give my soul the desired peace I desperately need,
chaotic thoughts continue to whirl in my mind,
over and over….
blackness encases me inside,
waves of repetitive uncertainty
continues to rattle my brain,
floating in this lake of darkness
I shiver from the lack of empathy and pain,
in the midst of losing my last hope,
the coldness reaches in hopes,
to pull me under the chilled slope,
holding my breath
I slowly surrender
to the emptiness inside,
as I let go I feel a warmth reach for my tattered body,
and unhurriedly surround me with *peace*,

a caress so inviting I feel intrigued to open my eyes,
blinded by a light so bright
and beautiful
the devil would feel
*love.*

# Hope

How can I change your evil heart of demise?
You loathe with disgust,
and regard revolting repugnance inside,
please take away the wrongful
hostility of detest in your eyes,
and please replace with deep
*affection* filled with infatuated *joy*,
look through the lens of the
heavens warm giving face,
with everlasting *hope*
and truthful *grace*,
please replace your hate and devise,
with peaceful ways
and with overflowing *love*
in your eyes.

# Patina

I dream of falling
from the heavens
like kaleidoscope raindrops,
pouring down like twinkling
iridescent hopes
of inspiring insights,
showering every rusty heart of pain,
washing away the corroded torture
of suffering.

# Spirit

*Energy* is all around us,
it's you,
it's me,
full of abundance,
it's passion, it's freedom,
it's fury inside,
it opens wounds you want to hide,
*blissful encounters,*
wash away the disease
flowing electric current awakens the soul to appease,
my body falls
and drops to my knees,
opening your consciousness to the world you see outside,
causes enlightened vitality to begin to see everything in a
*new light,*
colors are more vibrant
*crisp and clear,*

words ring differently in my ear,
my heart feels cured
healed and whole,
I let go of the hurt
and harmful incompleteness
of my *soul*.

# Daydream

I dream of a love so intense,
fire is envious
of our radiating impulses
of desire,
a magnetic connection
so intoxicating,
in our presence,
ecstasy is jealous.

# Window

*Encompassed* by a tantalizing
hypnotic gaze,
caressing every strand
of my body,
I desire eye contact so direct
I can feel an invisible envelopment
*intertwine* around every cell of my *spirit*,
locking eyes and watching
the intimate stare slowly devour me,
pulsating pleasure
evolving my *soul*,
throbbing to be touched.

# Embrace

Being *held* by you my pain
disintegrates inside,
I see the warmth and *love*
deep within your eyes,
please continue holding me
and never let me go,
I *love* the feel of *comfort*
I *hope* you truly know,
you can always imprison me
and detain me in your arms,
wrap me up close to you
shielding my body from harm,
you are my good luck *charm*
to me you'll always be,
so always hold me close to you
and continue *holding me*.

# Found

Why don't you *love* me,
I wonder as I stare,
but I already know the answer
in your eyes you don't care,
how can I be different,
I think to myself…
I can't, this is me,
so I go on without pout,
I'll be stronger without you,
I *promise* myself,
as I walk away from you,
I *love* the sound,
so don't come asking for me,
or come about,
I let you go years ago,
and now I'm *found*.

# Treasure Chest

*Unearth* my treasures
deep in my mind,
I welcome you in
to dig and find,
*excavate* my riches
buried in my intellect,
please come collect
don't reject,
*cherish* my valuables
I hide inside,
take them, I won't feel denied,
*gather* my gems
waiting to be found,
please don't leave them on the ground,
*hold* my jewels
I have internally,
or better yet
I'll give them to you personally.

# Endless Chatter

*"Why do I feel close yet so distant…*
*What went through your head just now?*
*Sorry because I missed it…"*
true communication
should never be a fad,
so please tell me what you're thinking
even if it's bad,
all I want is open communication,
*authentic,*
*raw,*
and *clear,*
not knowing what you are thinking
is what I fear,
so from this day forward
I promise to always be open and true,
so please *open your heart* to me
and I'll open mine to you.

# *Unconditional*

*Joy and laughter*
saved the day,
mended my broken heart away,
my fragmented center
overpowered with deep affection,
looking across at my *boys' direction*,
thank you so much for
your happiness and smiles,
my heart can literally
be heard for miles,
so from this day forward
I *promise* to be,
the best mother
a woman can be.

# Let Go

How do you let go
of bad feelings inside?
Like pain and anger,
that makes me want to run and hide,
I want to let go
of these feelings I feel,
I want *joy* to radiate
and bubble inside,
please help these bad feelings collide,
I want my body to jump and fly,
instead I want to break down and cry,
sometimes my empathy
feels like a curse,
I want to feel *happiness*
instead of the worst,
please help me, GOD,
take this away,
I want nothing more
than to *be okay*.

*Poetic Insights*

# Shine Bright

A wise friend of mine once said:
"There's no wrong way to feel,
but how you express ...."
let go of your bad feelings
and decompress,
breathe and observe,
the feeling instead,
let go of your bad feelings
in your head,
breathe in presence,
be here now,
it's all you have you must allow,
it's the true essence
of your existence,
you will achieve luminescence.

> # Synchronicity

I decided to *pray*
and said-
*"Let it be"*
and when I walked out
the clock read:


**333**

# Poetic Insights

# Soul Sister

I could tell instantly the
*truth* in your eyes,
you see things like I see
numbers and signs,
you make me *feel free*
and completely alive,
I know we may seem different
and come across as strange,
but we see things differently
and clearly
in a whole new arrange,
butterflies and hummingbirds,
clouds in the sky,
clouds that say "*I Love You*",
and make you want to cry,
you're my *soul sister* I coincide,
someone I'll always walk along with
I pinky swear,
*for life.*

# Calm

Discover your river
of *inner peace*,
letting your waterway
flow with ease,
a channel of *tranquility*,
solitude and seclusion,
I promise this is not an illusion,
*stillness* can turn into turbulent current,
rushing and crashing,
colliding with noise,
sit back *quietly* with pristine poise,
let your stream drift away,
soon you will be quiet again,
and *calm* at bay.

*Poetic Insights*

# Twin Flame

Back in *September of 2009*,
I felt an instant magnetic align,
I met a fine young man,
and hoped to make him mine,
maybe he'll ask me
to wine and dine,
tubing the Galaxie,
*sparks flew*,
making my feelings
a visual view,
*flickering particles*
making my heart skip a beat,
I couldn't wait to talk to him
he's so *sweet*,
nine months later
he was down on one knee,

*Laura Buck*

when I first met him
*I knew* from the start,
this was the man
*I'd always love,*
*with all of my heart.*

# Soul Mate

In a world full of chaos,
I want to look across and see you *anchored*
into my *solidified ground,*
fluffing your *nest*
in the resting place of my *heart,*
my welded roll cage covering my *soul,*
my firm *foundation* inside
my walls of anxiety,
encasing my *spirit* with
*calmness and serenity.*

# Wedding Day

I *hear* the melodious sweet-sounding
music playing inside,
*"Gift of a Thistle,"*
makes me want to cry,
tears of *happiness*
from the harmonious tune,
a favorite of mine, I always swoon,
joy embraces my anesthetizing body of nerves,
as I stand with my dad and wait
I truly feel my *true love state*,
I dreamt of this magical day all of my life,
to walk down the captivating aisle
and *become a wife*,
exhilarating excitement swirling in my soul
these thrilling emotions I can't control,
butterflies *pirouette* through the ecstatic essence
propelled by my thoughts of anticipation,
fluttering their sheer wings into a windy *nirvana*,
bagpipes hymn tones of blissful harmony,
sheathing my emotion with *thrilling melodic waves*,

*Poetic Insights*

*lifting my soul* into a dancing wonderland,
enhancing my body into midair heaven
treading closer to your presence,
*love* encases each valve
restoring my vitality with clarity
and *pure peace*,
rapid breaths overwhelm my lungs
intentionally I inhale *hopefulness*,
feeling it instantly enhance my being,
quickly I exhale my breath of *excitement*,
this is the moment
the moment I've waited for
all of my life,
the grand entrance will soon arrive,
I feel my *true love* awaiting me
watching the doors open I can see,
embraced by *love* and proud as can be,
in that moment I felt our souls intertwine
our *love collided*
yours and mine,
dad and I
side by side,
words ringing-
*"Here comes the bride!"*

# You

*You* don't need
another person viewing
and validating
your own gracious
embodiment of *you*.

If *you* need validation
for your own self-worth,
grace and dignity,
*you* already forfeited
your own *treaty to your soul*.

# Me

External approval
is no longer needed,
I don't need you
to understand me,
that took too long
to do it myself.

# Little Sis

I have a little sister
named *Kara Renae*,
she is so special to me in so many ways,
you *inspired* me to write again
without doubt,
you created a *fire* to burn
and not go out,
I feel you look up to me
wanting to hear the words from my soul,
you helped me *believe in me*
making me feel whole,
you make my heart sing
and dance to *Rock n' Roll*,

*Poetic Insights*

so when life is uncertain
and you need reassurance
in the night,
I hope my words soothe you
and hold you tight,
*"Always remember me*
*Little sis, okay?*
*Can you always be my rescuer*
*when I'm not okay?"*

# Mama & Papa

You both have the most *caring spirits*,
who always devotes your *compassionate*
souls to others before yourselves,
a *selfless love*,
you have the most genuine hearts
and are a true inspiration to me,
your *positive glow*
always draws others to you,
your loving nature
and *wholehearted adoration*
has helped me become the woman I am today,
you are my anchor
whom I look up to and call my *shining stars,*
you have given me the *roots* needed to always stay
*grounded* and taught me
to use my wings
to chase after my *dreams*.

# Silent Serenity

When I look at you,
I feel like you know how I feel,
I don't need to say anything
just *smile and heal*,
you know exactly what I'm thinking
and that's the real deal,
we have an *unspoken language*
only a few conceal,
we know more things than
others know,
we can't explain it, we just know
the feeling we feel is real inside,
we just have a *special bond*,
we can't deny.

# Cleanse

Wash my rusty heart of pain,
take away my tarnished strain,
cleanse my core, take away my stress,
disassemble my valves, make refreshed,
sweep my breast of corroded torture,
scrub my center back into working order,
wipe my middle oxidized stain,
polish my hub,
make it rain.

# Reflect

Meditation relieves my mind
releases tension that I find,
let go of every thought and let it be
give it to GOD and then you'll see,
every answer that you seek
is deep inside you if you peek,
letting go is hard to do
but don't give up
you'll soon see too.

# Inspire

*I know* I told you how much you
mean to me and why,
but there's more feelings
lingering deep inside,
you found the *hope* I needed to find,
you are my *anchor*
holding me grounded and tight,
you ignited a *flame*
I thought I lost inside,
you give me wings when I needed to take flight,
you are my *inspiration*
I needed to breathe,
now look at my *healed heart*
beneath my ribs of dreams.

# Moon Dance Mirage

I want to dance in prismatic
clouds of peace,
illuminated by sun rays of hope
lined with stardust and dreams,
floating in the comforts of the calm moonlight,
peaceful dreams encasing my soul,
twirling in a whirlwind of enchantment,
cascading a mystic silhouette of
swaying illusion.

# Golden Light

*Everything* is going to be okay
and unfold a better way,
there is no need to worry
live inside GOD's *glory*,
focus on the positive side
you *apply and decide*,
you can manifest anything you want,
it's pretty cool
don't act nonchalant,
do something you've never done
now your life has truly begun,
be someone you've never been
now you've found
the *light within*.

# *Poetic Insights*

# Life

*Thinking* of all the mistakes I've made
debts are due,
and left unpaid,
staring out in nature's wonder
What do I do,
I start to ponder,
I thought I had it all figured out
but I'm left with grief,
worry, and doubt,
What do I do,
I sit and *pray*,
*Universe*, I need you right now to display,
through sun rays and clouds of gray,
you show you're with me
in mysterious ways,
wind blows around me
within your *praise*,

bright shining light
in days of haze,
butterflies flying around me
in delight,
*Lord, I love You*
with all my might.

*Poetic Insights*

# Life Path # 7

I have a friend who
makes me *laugh* with glee,
every encounter
I'm nervous I'll pee,
every time you walk into a room
it *shines bright* as can be,
you wash away the hurt and pain
and make me feel free,
laughing hysterically
*feeling alive and brand new,*
all washed and shiny
only few can do,
hopping around
pretending in pain,
acting the part
feeling insane,

*I love you*, dear friend
forever you see,
never change who you are,
you are perfect for me,
so let's plan for forever,
*wild and free.*

# Magical Adventure

I prayed for a friend
and I know it's you,
I needed someone dearly
you are my glue,
I love when we are walking
and talking about stuff,
and thinking about our croissant sandwich
when we reach the top,
I love our walks filled with *good vibes*,
and the warm sun in our eyes,
I love our endless chats about art,
*kind words* fill my heart,
taking a break by a tree
drinking tea is where I want to be,
I love the freedom I feel with you,
Eagle Crest was the best view,

I'll never forget the exceptional place,
I was totally filled
with *magical grace*,
I'll walk with you
to the ends of the Earth,
always by your side,
"So where are we going next?
I'll drive."

# Twilight

Let GOD be the *anchor* to your soul,
welcome Him in
He'll make you whole,
He is everything
what you *wish* and what you need,
He loves you *unconditionally*,
so cast your worry and doubt to Him,
Don't be grim
He made your limb,
walking along the salty sea breeze,
*thankful* the heat
has come down some degrees,
washing my feet in the big blue sea,
twinkling and *smiling* at me,
tickling my toes,
I laugh with *delight*,

grounding my body
in the sand tonight
I walk along the surf twilight,
*Thank You* for loving me
and helping me find my light.

# Vow

On this day forward
I promise *me* to *you*,
to be the best version of *me*
I can be for *you*,
I'll pretend you're *me*
in hopes of vice versa too,
I'll be *me*,
the *me* you need,
and hopefully *you* will be
the *you* I need *you*
to be too.

# Rebirth

I'm an *old soul* full of emotions,
I overthink things and stare at the ocean,
I feel feelings deep to my center,
a empathic *kindred spirit*
and future mentor,
I'm full of knowledge and feelings unknown,
I've been reincarnated into several things,
living several lives into me brings,
*deep emotions* feelings and thoughts,
now I'm starting to connect the dots,
I've seen so many things in my *evolution*,
my feelings have feelings
I feel I have so many solutions,
I feel *empathy* deep to my core,
so many feelings and thoughts
I've felt and *explored.*

# Divine

*Open your heart* and you will see,
you're a prized possession
and free,
Have you heard of *Sotto Voce*?
It's up to you,
It's your choice,
*passionate* emotion filling my *soul*,
quilting my inner being
making me whole,
packing my psyche
with electrifying enchantment,
stuffing my *spirit* with
exhilarating commandment,
feeling carefree and completely alive
*gratitude* swirling inside,
the universe speaks to you
in so many ways,
open your heart to it
*sing in praise.*

# All As One

Natural beauty covers my eyes
with its *awe-inspiring* presentation,
I sit back and observe
GOD's beautiful foundation,
this place is vibrant
*spectacular and serene,*
I love the beauty being seen,
but something inside me tells me it's me,
I'm not just a person,
but this *magical scene,*
I feel the sun burning in my shirt,
my heart is buried deep in the dirt,
my soul is bound in the ground,
we are all *connected,*
to this *vision* you see,
I am you,
and you are me,
everything around me is me from my eyes,

# Poetic Insights

my *heart* continues beating
then I see with their *eyes*,
this is *remarkable*
in every generation,
seeing GOD's beauty
in all its *creation*.

# Sixth Sense

I *love* how you flow
through me,
the fluent *interpreted phrases*
of rhythmical insight,
flowing into my *healed soul*
with ease,
saturating my *awareness*
of spiritual intuition,
with comforting expressions of *hope*,
streaming magical scenes
into my world of *enchanting synchronicities*,
encased in a higher dimension of love,
full of impressive *imagination*.

# Buried Alive

Hard emotions bring me down,
pull me down into the ground,
I feel heavy,
weighing a ton,
*"Where is everyone?"*
Pressure encases me,
feeling buried and covered away,
I start to give up and say,
*"It's dark and confined,*
*Please unclog my airway!"*
I tense my muscles and try to relax,
this is not my death tax,
I'm not buried, I feel completely alive,
I've been planted,
I feel revived!!
I am growing,
I *survived*!!!

# Epilogue

I hope this book of poems shines a bright light for any soul needing to hear words of encouragement to know you are not alone. We all experience painful moments of heartache and pain. I hope the words written from my soul lift you out of the depths of the dark, giving you the peace and serenity needed to rise above the darkness and shine bright with love and understanding.

All my love,

Laura

# About The Author

Laura lives in Washington with her husband Bobby, and two boys, Kyler and Brayden. Laura loves to paint, and enjoys refurbishing furniture @thevintageitch . Stopping at her husband's shop at NW Bronco Fab and cruising around in a classic car is always a favorite pastime. When Laura has some free time she enjoys hiking with her best friend searching for the next waterfall in the beautiful Northwest. (The cover photo is her favorite falls, Falls Creek Falls.)

This is the first book Laura has written, and she strongly feels an intense overflow of enchanting energy motivated her to write these words. In just under two months Laura wrote all the poems in the book and had it published by TBN! Laura has always loved the delicate, rhythmical flow of enchanting words poetry creates. It's a language all its own. Laura said by writing down her feelings she received

a therapeutic gift and by translating her thoughts she
received a loving blessing from GOD, healing her broken

*soul.*

Printed in the USA
CPSIA information can be obtained
at www.ICGtesting.com
LVHW012215181123
764224LV00090B/4503